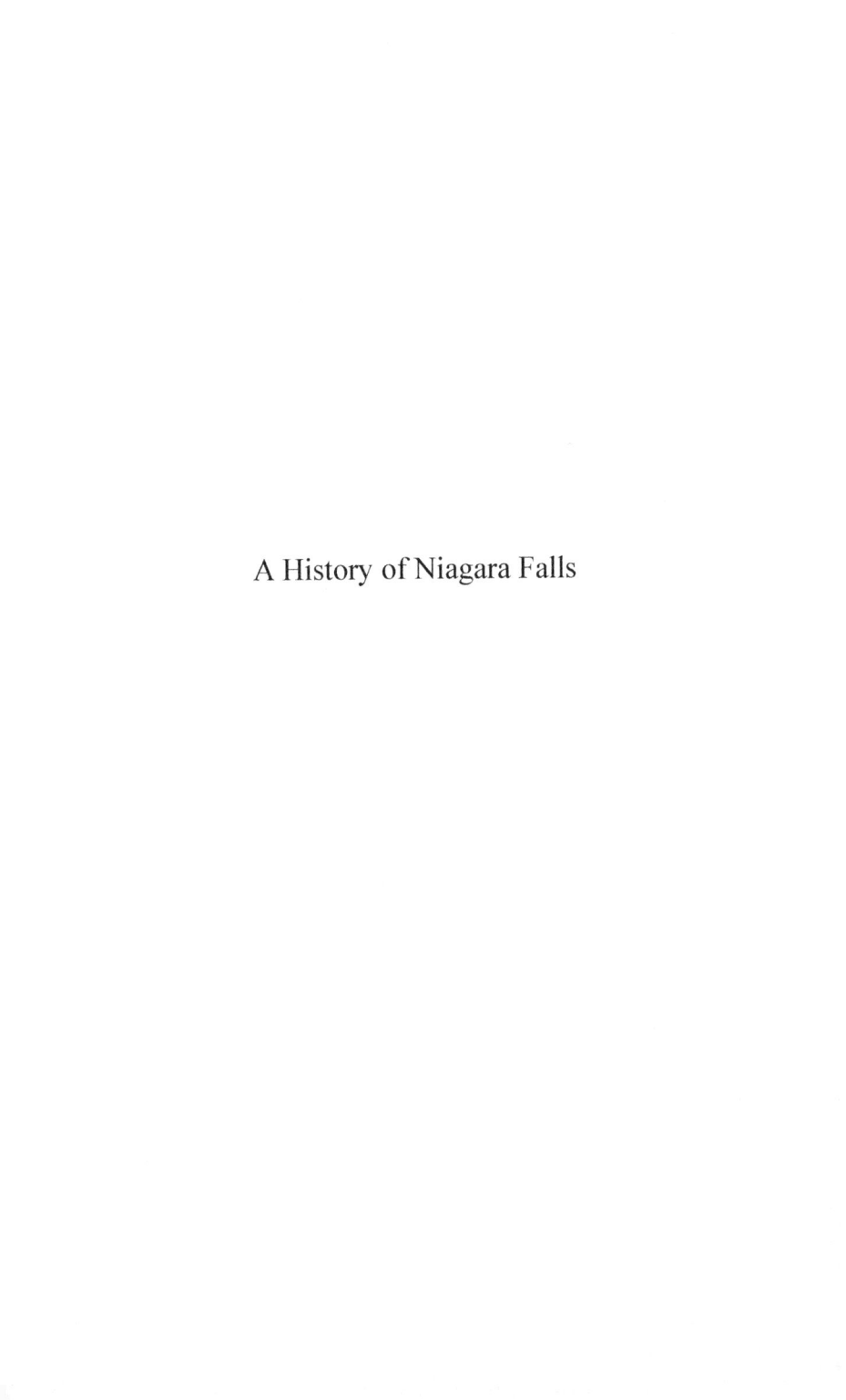

# A History of Niagara Falls

Prof. William D. Gunning
Dr John M. Clarke
Pr John Tyndall
G. Frederick Wright

# A History of Niagara Falls

LM Publishers

# The Past and Future of Niagara[1]

In October 1842, the Falls of Niagara were made the subject of careful study by the New York State Geologists. Under their direction a trigonometrical survey was made, and the river-banks—ancient and recent—the contours of Goat and Luna and Bath Islands, and the periphery of the Falls, were mapped with the utmost precision. The map is preserved in the archives of the State, at Albany, and the copper bolts and little stone monuments, which were placed to mark the trigonometrical points, remain—all, except those which fell with Table Rock. The American Association for the Advancement of Science, at its session last summer, petitioned the New York Legislature to provide for another survey. The expense would have been a mere trifle, but gentlemen of "the Reform Legislature" would not even consider the proposition. It is to be lamented, for another survey would give data by which we could translate into time nearly half a mile of the channel. Until the Falls shall be examined again by instrumentation, in estimating the rate of recession we must depend on the eye alone.

In 1840 old citizens told Lyell that the Falls recede about a yard in a year. I hear the same estimate from citizens now. They see a notch in the

---
[1] Prof. William D. Gunning

Horseshoe which was not there thirty years ago, and they see it growing deeper year by year; they see the American Fall more indented than it was when they used to observe it, and from such changes they construct a scale and apply it to the entire periphery. They deceive themselves. A careful study of the Falls from the trigonometrical points, even without instruments, and a comparison of what you see, with the map of 1842, would convince you that the recession during the past 30 years would fall inside of 15 feet. Let us take six inches a year as an approximation to the rate at which the Falls are eating back through the ledges of shale and limestone. The scale which answers to the last 30 years will apply to the channel from the Horseshoe to Ferry Landing, nearly half a mile. Through this part of the channel the Falls have cut through the same rocks they are cutting now. When they were at the site of Ferry Landing, a hard limestone, a member of the Clinton group, No. 4 of our section (Fig. 1), lay at their base, and the recession must have been arrested. Again, when they were at the site of the Whirlpool, a very hard, quartzose sandstone, marked 2 in the section, a member of the Medina system, lay at their base and checked their recession. Here the great cataract must have stood for ages almost stationary. With these two exceptions, the Falls, in every stage of their retreat, have cut through shale below, and the Niagara limestone above.

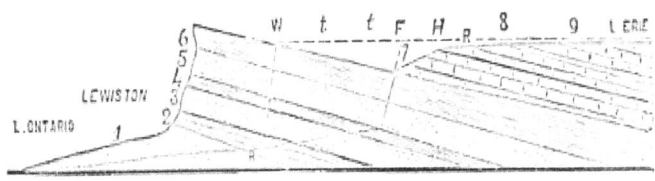

Section of Strata along the River from Lake to Lake
Fig.1. Numbers 1, 2, 3, belong to the Medina group; 4, to the Clinton group; 5, 6, 7, to the Niagara group; and S and 9 to the Onondaga group. Numbers 1 and 3 are red shaly sandstone; 2 is quartzose limestone; 4 green shale and limestone; 5 dark shale; and 6 gray limestone. W. site of the Whirlpool, where the Falls were 120 feet higher than now, and where their recession was checked by the quartzose sandstone, No. 2. The dotted line t, t, represents the highest terrace (or oldest riverbank) from the Whirlpool to the head of the Rapids, II. F represents the present site of the Falls, and B, E, the surface of the river from lake to lake.

Another element in the problem of Niagara's age is the flow of water. To construct a scale from the present and apply it to the past, we should know that the amount of water in past ages has been essentially the same as now.

About 9,800 cubic miles of water—nearly half the fresh water on the globe—are in the upper lakes, and 18,000,000 cubic feet of this plunge over Niagara Falls every minute, all the water of the lakes making the circuit of the Falls, the St. Lawrence, the ocean, vapor, rain, and lakes again, in 152 years. Through the Illinois Canal about 8,000 cubic feet of water are taken every minute from Lake Michigan to the Illinois River; through the Welland Canal 14,000 cubic feet flow every minute from Lake Erie into Lake Ontario, and through the Erie Canal 30,000 cubic feet pass every minute from the same lake into the Hudson. Thus, 52,000 cubic feet of water, which Nature would give to Niagara, are diverted every minute by artificial channels, some into the Mexican Gulf and some into the Bay of New York. Add this to 18,000,000, it is as a drop in the bucket, and would make no appreciable difference in the character of the Falls or their rate of recession. Was there ever a time when the Niagara was appreciably a greater river than now?

Below the Falls, on the Canada side, is a terrace, extending along the river-bank, and attaining a height of 46 feet. It contains river-shells, and is an old river-bank. A corresponding bank is found on the New York side, although much broken and eroded. If a tourist will stand on the New Suspension Bridge and cast his eye along these ancient banks, his first impression will be that the Niagara which flowed against them was vastly greater than the river which flows now nearly 200 feet below him. But, if his eye will follow the Canadian terrace above the Horseshoe, he will see it falling lower and lower, till, at the head of the Rapids, it merges into the present bank. From this point upward the river is contained within low banks, and bounded by a plain whose monotony is not broken by a hill or terrace. A glance at the section (Fig. 1) will make this clear to the eye of the reader. The surface of the river from Buffalo to Lake Ontario is represented by the line R, R; the banks, from Buffalo to the Rapids, by the dotted line t, t and the *old* banks, from the Rapids to the Whirlpool, by a continuation of the same line. It will be seen that this line rises as the surface of the river falls. The slope from the head of the Rapids to the Falls is nearly 50 feet, and the terrace opposite the Falls attains a height of 46 feet.

We turn now to Goat Island. A walk around the island, by the margin of the river, will show us what immense denudation its limestones have suffered. The extent of this denudation can be seen in our section of the island (Fig. 2). To wear away such beds of limestone, the river, for many ages, must have flowed over the island. And as the upper beds of fluviatile drift, marked, d in our section, are a little below the level of the highest terrace, we must infer that the river, when contained in these ancient banks, covered the island, and was eroding its beds of limestone.

By all this we see that the Niagara itself has made the Rapids, and that, as it cut its way downward, its forsaken banks have assumed the character of terraces. And we see, by the low banks and absence of old banks above the Rapids, that even the highest of these ancient banks did not contain a greater river than this which flows through the narrow gorge today.

We assume, then, from all the monuments the river has left of its own history, that the present rate of recession would be a fair measure of the past, except at the Whirlpool and Ferry Landing. Six inches a year, measured on the channel, would place the Falls at Lewiston 74,000 years ago. We have no means of knowing how long the quartzose sandstone, which forms the lowest part of the bank at the Whirlpool, would have arrested the cataract. This stratum is 25 feet thick, and, as its southward dip is 20 feet a mile, and the slope of the river-channel 15 feet a mile, the Falls would have to cut back through this rock more than half a mile. The halt may have been many thousand years. Add another period for the halt at the landing, and the age of the channel, from Lewiston to the Horseshoe, may not fall below 200,000 years. Unquestionably the channel has been excavated since the close of the glacial epoch, which science has well-nigh demonstrated occurred about 200,000 years ago. But this channel is only the last chapter in the history of Niagara.

Fig. 2.

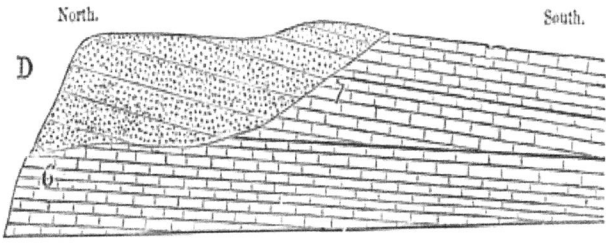

SECTION OF GOAT ISLAND

No. 6, the Niagara limestone (6 also of Fig. 1); No. 7, the shaly limestone (marked 7 in Fig. 1). The Rapids have been formed by the erosion of this limestone. D, alluvial drift covering the eroded limestone. The section will show how great had been the denudation of the limestone by the river before the drift D accumulated, and before the river had found its present level.

Standing by the Whirlpool on the east, and looking over the river, we see a break in the ledges of rock which everywhere else form the bank. On the western side, around the bend of the Whirlpool, for a distance of 500 feet, bowlders and gravel take the place of ledges of rock. Many of these bowlders are granite and greenstone and gneiss, which have travelled hundreds of miles from the northeast. This mass of northern drift fills an old river-channel, which we can trace from the Whirlpool to the foot of the escarpment at St. David's—about two miles and a half. The reader will see by the map (Fig. 4) that this old channel marked 13 lies in a line with the present channel above the Whirlpool. The opening at St. David's is two miles wide. Here the Falls stood "in the beginning," wide, but not deep. They had cut back two miles and a half when the glacial period came, and lakes and rivers, and the great cataract, were buried under a colossal sheet of ice. If we can trust astronomical data (Stone's Tables of the Eccentricity of the Earth's Orbit), the glacial epoch lasted about 50,000 years. Add this to the age of the present channel, and 25,000 years for the preglacial channel, and we have 275,000 years as an approximation to the age of Niagara River.

Of course these figures are given merely as an approximation to the truth. To the general reader the time seems immense. But to the geologist it seems short, and his concern is to account for the æons in which the lakes and their water-shed must have stood above the ocean, but which the Niagara has not registered. Let us attend for a little while to the earlier history of this Niagara region.

From the Old Suspension Bridge three geologic systems can be seen on the river-banks. The lowest is a red, mottled, shaly sandstone, the *Medina sandstone*. It is marked 3 on the section (Fig. 1). Above this, and having the same dip, is a thin group of green shale and gray limestone, the *Clinton group*, No. 4 of the section. Overlying the Clinton is dark shale, and over the shale a thick band of gray limestone, the two forming the *Niagara group*, designated on the section by Nos. 5 and 6.

Below the escarpment at Lewiston, as the diagram will show, the lowest member of the Medina sandstone (No. 1, Fig. 1) appears as the surface rock. We find it ripple-marked and carrying the *Lingida cuneata* and *Fucoides Harlani*, its characteristic shell and seaweed. It underlies a good part of Western New York and Canada, and extends southward into Pennsylvania and Virginia, with everywhere the same characters, indicating a quiet, shallow sea, fed by rivers which for ages brought down the same sediments. It is eighth in the series of palaeozoic rocks which form the first volume of the world's history after the beginnings of life, and is the oldest rock which shows itself about the Falls.

Up the river, about two miles from Lewiston, the railroad, which descends the river-bank, takes us to the junction of the Medina sandstone with the Clinton group. The green shale is barren here, but at Lockport we have found it full of *Agnostics lotus*, a little ill-defined crustacean. The overlying limestone is exceedingly rich in fossils, *Atrypa neglecta* being the characteristic shell. The sea had changed both its life and the rock material on its bottom.

Another change, and to the Clinton succeeded the Niagara period. The change was not abrupt, for many species, common in the Clinton sea, lived in the Niagara as well.

In the Niagara shale we have found *Conularia Niagarensis*, a shell which must be referred to a Pteropod mollusk. Pteropods of the living world are seen only on mid-ocean. They flap themselves over the water by wing-like appendages from the side to the head. Their shells do not drift ashore, but the dredge has brought them up from the ooze of the deep-sea bottom. Now, this Niagara shale is only the hardened ooze of an ancient sea-bottom, and the *Conularia* tells us that here the sea was open and deep.

A time came when mud-sediments were no longer brought down, and the bottom of an ocean, clear, warm, placid, over an area which extended from the Hudson far beyond the Mississippi, was a vast grove of coral. In sheltered nooks of the coral-grove were gardens of waving crinoids, and three-lobed, many-jointed, many-eyed trilobites were crawling over the coral sand, and mollusks in richly-sculptured shells were everywhere on sand and coral. The Niagara limestone is a monument of that ancient life. With the formation of this rock and its uplift from the sea, the geologic record here about Niagara closed, until the coming of the Ice.

We turn now to the geology of the lake-region. The area of the lakes is estimated at 90,000 square miles; and the area whose streams flow into the lakes, at 400,000 square miles. This immense area is one of the oldest on the globe. On the north shore of Lake Huron and Lake Superior we find the azoic rocks, and on the borders of Lake Erie and Lake Michigan we find no rock newer than the lowest members of the Devonian. The whole water-shed of the St. Lawrence was reclaimed from the ocean before the close of the Devonian epoch. If the drainage has always been through the gulf of St. Lawrence, the Niagara should be one of the oldest rivers on the globe. And yet, as we have seen, in the geological calendar it is very young. How shall we account for this gap between ocean-history and river-history? A little more of geology and something of topography will help us to understand why the Niagara has recorded such a small segment of the time which lies between us and the Devonian seas.

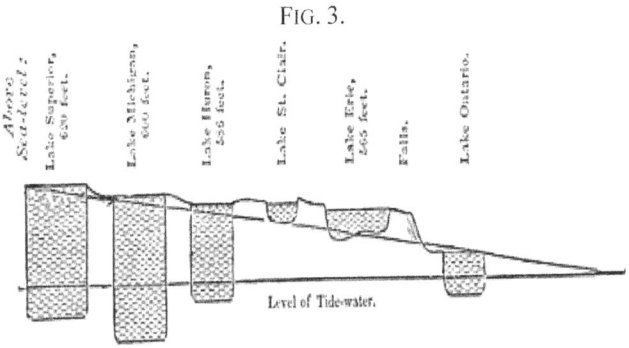

Hypotenuse of the Triangle, 1,600 Miles long.
IDEAL SECTION OF THE ST. LAWRENCE AND ITS LAKES.

Borings made a few years ago at La Salle, on the Illinois, revealed the fact that the valley had been eroded forty feet below the present river-bed. Potholes and water-worn ledges at Athens mark the course of an ancient river. Other evidences of the ancient river are found in the valley of the Des Plaines and along the Calumet feeder of the Illinois Canal.

The topography of the lake-basins and the Niagara plateau will explain that old river-bed.

Lake Erie, as everybody knows, and as we have indicated in the ideal section of the St. Lawrence and its lakes (Fig. 3), fills a shallow basin eroded in a plateau 333 feet above the level of Lake Ontario, and 565 feet above the ocean. The surface of Lake Michigan is 600 feet above tide-level, and, as the lake is 1,000 feet deep, its bottom is 400 feet below the level of tide-water. Lake Superior is 900 feet deep, and its surface about 20 feet above that of Lake Michigan. The Niagara, from Buffalo to the head of the Rapids, has a fall of 15 feet. The fall from Lake Michigan to Goat Island is 50 feet—just equal to the slope of the Rapids. A barrier 15 feet high, stretching across the plateau at the head of the Rapids, would throw the river back on Lake Erie, and such a barrier, 50 feet high, would hold back the waters of Lake Michigan.

We can see the significance, now, of a few features of topography about the Falls.

The reader will turn to the map of Niagara River, which we have drawn, with some modifications, from the official maps of the Boundary Commission. He will see that, from the foot of Grand Island to the Falls, the course of the river is almost due west. At the Falls it makes an elbow, and extends thence, with no abrupt winding except at the Whirlpool, northward to Lake Ontario. At Schlosser Landing, about a mile above the Rapids, a stream called Gill Creek empties into the river. It is not more than six miles long, and its course is parallel to that of Niagara below the Falls. Its source is a swamp about two miles east of the river, and nearly the same distance north of Old Fort Gray. We have the anomaly of two streams flowing side by side, within two miles of each other, in opposite directions, and through an apparently level country. Gill Creek, flowing southward, has a fall in six miles, of 60 feet. Its source is 60 feet higher than the surface of Niagara at Schlosser Landing. This high land is not a hill, but a ridge—an anticlinal axis extending from northeast to southwest across the Niagara channels. Before it was broken through and eroded, it formed a barrier a few feet higher than the surface of Lake Michigan. Then Niagara was not, and the upper lakes sought the ocean through a great river, sections of whose channel, as we have seen, can still be traced from Chicago to the Illinois.

FIG. 4.

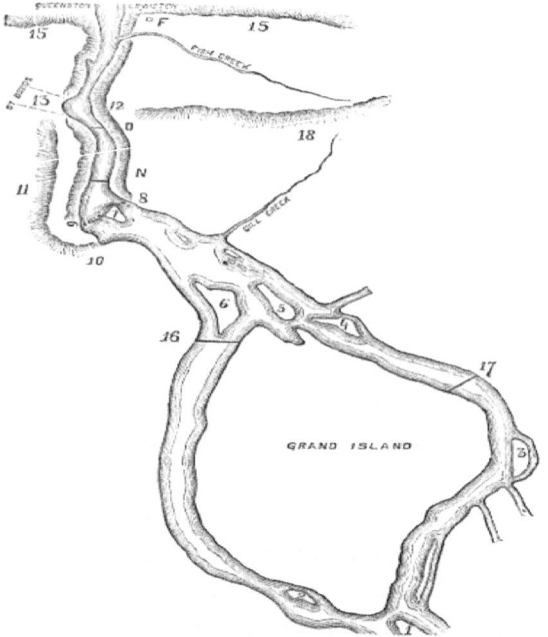

MAP OF THE REGION OR NIAGARA FALLS.

1. Strawberry Island; 2. Beaver Island; 3. Tonawanda Island; 4. Cayuga Island; 5. Brockton Island; 6. Navy Island; 7. Goat Island; 8. American Fall; 9. Horseshoe Fall; 10. Gas Spring; 11. Oldest Terrace; 12. Whirlpool; 13. Preglacial Channel; 15, 15. Line of the Escarpment; N. New Suspension Bridge; O. Old Suspension Bridge; F. Fast Ground; 16, 17. Position of the Falls when the shale shall dip below the river-bed, and the limestone shall form the entire precipice. After receding so fur, the Falls will then wear away into cascades and rapids. 18. The Old Barrier.

We have lingered long in the past. What of the future? The intelligent tourist who stands by the great cataract cannot allow the beauty, the grandeur, the vast magnificence of the scene, to bear down his imagination and bind up all his powers in the present. He looks and listens, and, while he stands overpowered by the falling torrent and rising spray, and thunderous pounding of torrent on fallen torrent, his imagination breaks the spell, and his thoughts wander away into the past and the yet to be. Are future ages to see this wonder, and find it as great as our eyes see it?

Mr. Hall, in his report on the Fourth District, and Sir Charles Lyell, in his "First Travels in the United States," have told us what they thought the Falls are coming to.

The reader will remember that the dip of the strata here is 20 feet a mile *southward*. He will remember, too, that the current below the Falls is 15 feet a mile northward. If he will turn to the section it may help him to see that a stratum which, a mile below the Falls, crops out along the bank 35 feet above the river, would be brought down, at the Falls, to the level of the river; and he will see that, for every mile the Falls have cut their way southward, they have lost 35 feet in height—the dip of the strata and slope of the channel. Let them cut back two miles farther (this is the reasoning of Hall and Lyell), and they will have passed the head of the Rapids. The shale which now lies at their base and forms the lower part of the precipice will have disappeared beneath the river-bed, and the limestone which has always been at the top of the precipice will have reached the bottom. As the Falls have receded by the action of the spray on the shale below, and the breaking and falling down of the undermined limestone above, now that the entire precipice is limestone, the features of the cataract will begin to change. The rock will wear away faster at the top than at the bottom, and the great Niagara—only a hundred feet high now—will dwindle away into a succession of cascades and rapids. This is the future as shaped in the minds of Hall and Lyell. They have overlooked an important fact the change in the course of the river.

A reference to the map will show that the American Fall (8) is cutting eastward, and the Horseshoe (9) southward. But, after a few hundred feet have been cut away, the direction of the Horseshoe will change, and both Falls will move *eastward*. Above Goat Island they will unite and move on, one Fall, of immense width, till Navy Island cuts it in two. The greater Fall will then be on the American side, and its recession will still be eastward. A little Fall on the Canada Bide will retreat southward around Navy Island and then Grand Island. About a mile above the northern point of Grand Island this Fall will have moved southward far enough to leave the shale and have the precipice all of limestone. The water will then wear away the rim faster than the base, and the Fall will become a series of cascades and rapids.

But the main Fall will have to cut back to within a mile of Tonawanda Island—by the course of the river, nearly eight miles from the Horseshoe before it makes the same southing. The Fall will have cut back, not *with* the dip, but nearly at right angles *across* it. And by the present rate of recession it must continue its work of excavation for 80,000 years before the shale will disappear under the bed of the river and the limestone form the entire precipice. Then the same fate will overtake this greater Fall which, ages before, awaited the other. All this on the assumption that Nature is to go on selecting her own channels and seeking her own ends.

But man is, here, greater as a mere dynamic than any other force acting on the globe. Already Niagara has felt his power. Fifty-two thousand cubic feet of water which belong to her, every summer minute be diverts to his own uses. Another century will see him on every acre along the borders of the upper lakes. Every forest he fells, every acre he ploughs, will affect, though inappreciably, the flow of water over the Falls. Time may come when his hand, laid on the earth in gigantic enterprise, will cause the Falls to shrink into insignificance. He will make these lakes furnish him highways to the ocean, east and south. A canal from Lake Michigan to the Illinois, great enough to float ships laden for the marts of Europe, and another from Lake Erie to Lake Ontario, are achievements in the near future.

# The Menace to Niagara[2]

Forecasts by eminent geologists of the future of Niagara Falls have been much in the public eye and have lost some of their novelty though none of their interest. The great cataract, it is said, is committing suicide, and the physical factors which enter into the process have, it is thought, been carefully weighed. If matters proceed as they are now going, the face of the cataract receding without interruption, the falls are to wear themselves out, or if the dominating crustal movement continues, the escarpment is to be left bare because its waters will be stolen away and turned back into Lake Erie.

These are interesting possibilities, but they hardly rise to the dignity of probabilities, for opposing considerations have been left out of the calculations and even the remote periods assigned to their arrival grow longer and more distant in the face of factors overlooked or not sufficiently estimated. Nothing can be as wrong as mathematics or logic where the premises are wrong; nothing more excusable than the trial forecast for the life of a spectacular natural phenomenon, even though it will be and remain improbable till every factor in play has been given its full share in the process.

The problem of Niagara is not simple. As one sees with each change of the sun a new wonder in

---
[2] By Dr John M. Clarke

its fascinating rush of waters, so every reconsideration of the problem of its natural future brings into activity contributory and qualifying elements before unrecognized.

The intelligent public, now quite familiar with these forecasts, looks upon the Niagara cataract as doomed at some remote time and from causes which human power cannot control, and doubtless this feeling, now that the novelty of the sensation is past, has been followed by an intellectual resignation. Even the claims of posterity, the passing pang that our descendants may not see the mighty cadence of water as our eyes see it, quite relax all hold upon us in view of the fact that after all this may not happen just as represented.

The heavy bed of tough dolomite limestone at the crest of the falls, which is the occasion of their existence, lies above a thick mass of soft shale which easily caves in under the rebound of the falling waters, and by so doing becomes the chief cause of the breaking down of the crest and of the cataract's retreat. This bed of shale runs down into the earth in the direction from which the water comes, the south. It will be out of the reach of the cataract after a while, leaving an escarpment wholly composed of the tough limestone, which will make the problem of retreat thenceforward quite a different one from what it is today. There are, moreover, fifty-seven feet of hard dolomites above the crest of the falls over whose edges the water now descends in rapids. As the cataract moves southward by the falling away of its rock face it will grow higher instead of lower, until after it has passed the parting of the waters above Goat Island. Indeed it may become fifty feet higher than it now is and so firmly upheld by the heavy masonry of limestones that caving in must cease and further retreat will be reduced to its slowest terms.

As to the crustal movement whose tendency is to spill the waters westward out of the Erie basin, Ave may observe that the earth's crust is most uneasy and its movements most uncertain. Nearly every place is going either up or down, few are in a state of actual quietude. These movements have every variety of period; some may be secular, some are known to be relatively brief. Fifty years ago the shore at Perce on the Gaspe coast was going down, the fishermen had to abandon their drying stages and build them farther up the beach, but to-day the shore is coming up again and excavations for the new stages reveal the remains of the old ones which have been buried in the sea for nearly two generations. There is no knowing when the movement now affecting the Niagara region will cease.

Public resignation over the natural but distant fate of Niagara has grown to public concern at its immediate future. It is alleged that the present and contemplated industrial development at Niagara Falls immediately imperils the integrity and perpetuity of that great spectacle. Is this true? If it is, the American and Canadian public who hold this phenomenon in trust for the world ought to know it. However this question may be received and however answered by the interested producer or the disinterested public, it has on more than one occasion been flatly and formally before the people of the State of New York and of the Province of Ontario and has had to be met.

The legislative bodies of these two governments must meet it again, for it is plainly not the present temper of the public to let it pass in uncertainty.

Any citizen of New York or Ontario may justly take a pride in the magnificent industrial development building up about Niagara Falls, even though it is all at the cost of the beauty and magnificence of the cataract. Nowhere else has nature afforded such tremendous power at once available to mankind and calling forth the highest play of his genius. If I could hold a brief for the development of these natural resources it would be the delight of my pen to paint the wealth, the contributions to human comfort which will flow from them. I might argue that nature created this tremendous fall of water for the express purpose of contributing to commercial power and industrial supremacy. Such a brief would lament, as I have heard a distinguished engineer lament, the actual waste of power during the ages in which the great river has been discharging itself in unutterable glory and construe it sinful to neglect the opportunity so lavishly afforded. Such a brief might deride and cachinnate at the possibility of ever diverting enough water from Niagara to make the Falls palpably less, and all these arguments it would not be difficult to enforce with specious reasoning and pleading facts.

The attitude of the man who is willing and ready to see Niagara entirely drained for the wealth it would produce, and only a dreary canyon left to speak of its splendid past, is wholly intelligible, or would be except for the potent facts that wealth and happiness and contentment are purely relative and that the natural forces of the world were not created for the use of man.

The question I have put has been not only asked, but answered in New York, officially. The abstraction of water from Niagara Falls was condemned by a committee of the constitutional convention appointed to investigate this subject in 1894, when the public had begun to suspect that the legislature had been too free with its gifts of franchises to power companies. It was vigorously and effectively answered by Governor Odell in 1901, who stood out finely against a tremendous pressure brought to bear upon him by the industrial interests, not through any hostility to them, but for the simple sentimental reason that the Falls must be conserved. Few know the courage of this act, but it was a triumph of sentiment and morality which the citizens of New York may well applaud.

The editor of the Popular Science Monthly has asked me to set forth the facts relating to the situation at Niagara Falls in such form that it may be made clear whether existing and impending conditions there constitute an actual menace to the cataract and its accompanying attractions, or whether public apprehension has been unnecessarily aroused by a kind of pantophobia which may work a real injustice to industrial progress.

Except for that slender radical element of the community which proudly avows its willingness to see the Falls wholly developed into power all will agree that if danger is impending to the cataract it is time now that the danger be measured and fully apprehended.

The conservation of Niagara Falls is a question of public morals. Every industrial enterprise of wide scope has as its foundation a moral problem ; it cannot be simply the producer of great wealth regardless of the rights of others and of the higher claims of community life ; nor can it ignore the claims of spiritual excellence and of the higher life which seeks something beyond the minted ideal. This claim of the higher life, the demands of the finer emotions, the love for the beautiful in nature, express themselves in part in the government protection of natural wonders from defacement and destruction; in organizations created to keep alive this sentiment and extend the aegis of the state over natural glories which belong to mankind rather than to men. No wise man confesses himself devoid of such emotions.

The violation of this moral principle in present practise offends the best sentiments of the race. It is said that the classic Falls of Lodore have been done to death by conversion into power. The far-famed Falls of Montmorency at Quebec show only a tremulous and weakened front to the traveler on the St. Lawrence, shorn of their glories in order to light the City of Quebec. The City of Rochester, seat of learning, refinement and industrial achievement, has exchanged the beautiful cascades of the Genesee for a slimy canyon. These attacks on natural phenomena have benefited the few, contributed to their comfort and convenience; they have injured the many, robbed them of a natural and proper heritage.

Under the guidance of this principle the claim of the individual, personal or corporate, must give way to the broadly founded rights of the community and the race. Under whatever political control such a majestic demonstration of nature's power may be, this control must be looked upon as a trust rather than the possession of a merchantable commodity or a commercial asset. States have not the moral right to do as they please with such phenomena. In a final analysis the individual or corporate claim to advantage from such a source is wholly extinguished, howsoever expediency may qualify and adjust the conflicting claims.

Wherein does the danger to Niagara Falls from industrial development lie? Simply in the drawing off of its waters from the river above the cataract, carrying them around the cliff by some other way or discharging them by tunnel into the face of the falls near the base.

The use of Niagara waters for power production has been the dream of years and its earliest successful achievement is expressed in the present

Niagara Falls Hydraulic Power & Manufacturing Co., whose existence as an active consumer of Niagara water antedates its statutory recognition. The legislature of New York began giving away franchises to power companies about twenty years ago. It has never asked a financial return of any sort for any of these, as, during the period from 1885 to 1894, when they were most freely granted, it probably seemed not wise to inflict a revenue on a budding industry. New York thus receives nothing whatever in return for the privileges it has granted for the consumption of its own waters. We mention this fact incidentally, just as we may mention that the Canadian companies are to pay a substantial return for similar privileges; but this matter of revenue has no bearing whatever on the theme before us. Whether or not any public revenue be derived from the use of Niagara is entirely beside the issue save as taxation of the product of the companies can be used as a means for the control of the situation.

The American Channel at the Crest of the Falls during the Ice Jam of March, 1903.

Nine of these companies have been legally recognized or chartered in New York. Of these charters, all were granted in good faith, but it may be doubted if all were asked for and received in the same spirit. Some, it would seem, were immediately for sale as soon as granted. Some failed to effect organization because the present requirements of such an undertaking demand enormous capital.

A VIEW OF THE AMERICAN BANK, SHOWING THE POWER-HOUSE OF THE N. F. H. P. AND M. CO., THE ENCLOSED TAIL-RACES AND THE GROWING ROW OF STRUCTURES AT THE EDGE OF THE WATER.

Some were limited in respect to the amount of water they may abstract from the river, as the Niagara Falls Hydraulic Power & Manufacturing Co., to 462,000 cubic feet per minute, and the Niagara Falls Power Co., to 516,000 cubic feet per minute. Others were restricted in the amount of power to be produced, as the last named company, which may not exceed 200,000 horse-power. In most cases, however, no limitations were placed either on power to be produced or water to be abstracted. Several were limited as to the time in which they were to begin work in good faith, two of them to five years, two to ten years. Three if not four of the charters are dead by limitation, one company sold its franchise to another, one is slumbering with an occasional show of life, another is leading a questionable life and two are producing and selling power.

The American Bank below the Steel Arch Bridge, showing the waste of water and power from the spillways and tail-races of the factories.

The Niagara Falls Hydraulic Power & Manufacturing Co. and the Niagara Falls Power Co., the productive organizations, are alone to be credited with the really amazing industrial developments at this place, and they are still far within their statutory limitations in the consumption of water. With this superb display of mechanical achievement before his eyes one looks and looks in vain for a depauperated and enfeebled cataract. The flow of water is of course diminished, but to the occasional visitor it is but mathematically perceptible.

Citizens of Niagara Falls who have the cataract daily before the eye have insisted that the loss of water is perceptible, and that such loss is felt in other ways is seen in the now annual gorging of the ice in the American channel at the upper end of Goat Island, which lays bare the American channel, sends all its water to Canada, and which very rarely happened when the depth of the water was normal.

The two active American companies are not going to use any less water than now, but are vigorously increasing their output and building new power houses to meet their growing market. Indeed, one of them, realizing its close approach to statutory limits, has established itself on the Canadian side. These two companies are permitted to consume the following amounts of water:

Niagara Falls Hydraulic Power & Manufacturing Co ............................................ 7,700 cu. ft. per sec.
Niagara Falls Power Co ............. 8,600 "

The water abstracted by these companies is in no small degree wasted, that is to say the power produced is no equable measure of the amount of water taken from the river. This page carries a picture familiar to a thousand eyes — the view of the American bank below the steel arch bridge. This has been termed ' the backyard view of Niagara. The little cascades springing from holes in the side of the bank at various heights are the wasteways of the factories above. Some of these cascades are now encased in flumes and made productive at the bottom of the cliff, but this is only a recent change designed to save the wasted power, but involving the construction of a row of factories or wheel pits all along the edge of the water. The fall from the height of waters where these two companies have their intakes, to the base of the cataract, is approximately 224 feet, far beyond the working possibility of the turbine pit. The outrush of water at the base of the cliff near the bridge anchorage is the discharge of the great tunnel of the Niagara Falls Power Co., which is the tail-race from the wheel pits far back up the city and far above in the rocks.

On the Canadian side the activity in the erection of power works has been more strenuous. Utter devastation of the natural beauties of Queen Victoria Park, the demolition of islands and creeks, the excavation of the rock surface to the complete obliteration of well-known landmarks, have been the accompaniments of the unparalleled endeavors and achievements here. Whoever has visited this part of the Falls region since the beginning of these gigantic operations has sought in vain for the Dufferin Islands and Crescent Island, and what must have seemed to him an inextricable chaos of rock excavations, of switches and sidings, of temporary and permanent constructions, in confusion worse confounded, has confronted him. Out of it all, it is presumed, the plans for the *artificial* beautifying of the spot will gradually unfold and the visitor of coming years is to see it with its attractions not only restored,' but enhanced.

Great sections of the river bottom, acres of rock over which the river has flowed for ages in tumultuous energy, have been for the first time exposed to the eye of man and the light of the sun. These sections of the river have now in large part been absorbed into forebays and intakes, into the permanent constructions of the companies, never to be given back to their proper charge.

Site of the Power-house of the Ontario Power Company at the Edge of the Water below the Falls on the Canadian Side.

The three Canadian companies are to be greater consumers than the American. They are the finest, the most magnificent conceptions of hydraulic engineering, and in their ultimate realization rise to proportions which are an expression of the genius that has inspired them. No one of these, let us remark, is moribund or inactive; each shows the highest type of virility.

| | | |
|---|---|---|
| The Canadian Niagara Power Co. has a statutory limit of consumption of | 8.900 | cu. ft. per sec. |
| The Ontario Power Co. | 12.000 | "□" |
| The Toronto & Niagara Power Co. | 11,200 | "□" |
| | 32,100 | "□" |

Adding to this total the limits of the American producing companies (16,300), we have for the entire chartered abstraction of the five companies referred to, 48,400 cubic feet per second.

This is of itself a dry and apparently barren fact. Let us look to its bearings upon the structure of the Niagara River and the total flow of waters through its channel.

The Niagara River flows over a rock bottom, on which the strata dip uniformly to the west. The sill or edge of the Falls is ten feet higher on the American than on the Canadian side, the waters at the crest of the American Falls ten feet shallower.

The Rock-bed of the River on the Canadian Side, now partly enclosed by Permanent Construction.

The flow of water through the channel and over the Falls was measured by the United States engineers in 1868, and by Sir Casimir Gzowski in 1870-3, with results varying from 246,000 cubic feet per second (the latter) to a maximum of 280,000 cubic feet per second (the former). The later averages given by the United States engineers, derived from the mean flow of water from Lake Erie at Buffalo during a period of forty years, afford 222,400 cubic feet per second. There are certain constants of abstraction for the Welland and the Erie canals which may be regarded as equalized by the inflow of streams into the river between Buffalo and the Falls, so that the figure which has been generally accepted and has entered into the calculations of the engineers is 224,000 cubic feet per second. It is in cubic feet per second that we prefer to express our statements; the attempt to put them in terms of horse-power is attended with too many uncertainties.

The potential or theoretical horse-power of this volume of water falling in the cataract is variously, sometimes carelessly stated in the engineers' reports as from three to six millions. A recalculation gives it at 3,800,000 for the cataract, which would be increased by the additional fall from the height of the rapids to the crest of the Falls. Goat Island, picketing the frontier, divides the waters unfairly, giving much more than three-fourths of their volume to the Canadian side, though the international boundary established by the Treaty of Ghent lies at the line of deepest water. Now as less than one fourth of the total volume of the waters pours down the American channel and this channel is much shallower than the other, it is at once evident that abstractions of water will make themselves first perceptible in the shoaling of the American channel. At the parting of the waters above Goat Island the great current of the river moves to the west, and converges into the funnel of the splendid Horseshoe Falls.

The Rock-bed of the River, left Dry by the Wing Dam of one of the Canadian Companies.


The American channel actually carries in comparison but a feeble flow and the whole American cataract is in extremely delicate equilibrium. A competent hydraulic engineer, taking the accepted volume of the flow, the length of the entire crest of the Falls on both sides (4,070 feet) and the difference in elevation of the sill of the Falls, has calculated that when the flow is reduced to 184,000 cubic feet per second, or by 40,000 cubic feet, the water will be down to the present rock bottom at the edge of the American shore.

Wing Dam of one of the Canadian Companies running out to the Edge of the Rapids.

Then the American Falls, though still forming a cataract, will be but a ghost of their ancient magnificence; instead of the mighty sheet of emerald waters now spreading in silent majesty over the rock crest, a weakly, thin, white apron of waters carried forward by a slender impulse *a tergo* and the great cadence will have lost its glory. Electric searchlights in all the colors of the rainbow dancing up and over the falling waters and other factitious means of producing a spectacle will never compensate the loss.

Let one fifth more of the water be abstracted beyond the line we have already calculated and the

American channel will be dry. That is, in effect, double the amount of 40,000 cubic feet, and when 80,000 cubic feet have been taken away from the present flow the Canadian channel will still be an interesting object, but the American Falls will be wholly gone.

All our figures in these statements and calculations, it may be well to repeat, are taken from the reports of the United States engineers, of the power companies' engineers, or have been specially derived at my solicitation by engineers of high standing.

We may return to the data given concerning present and immediately contemplated abstraction.

The two American and three Canadian companies now in operation or about to operate, when producing to their charter limits will abstract 48,000 cubic feet per second. That amount will bring the water-level to the bottom of the river at the American shore.

So much then is in immediate prospect. The turning of the waters a few days ago into the largest turbines the world has ever seen, thus inaugurating the actual production of Canadian power, sounded the death knell of the American Falls, leaving to those whose hearts sink and whose spirits shrivel at the thought of this destruction only a slender hope that it may be mechanically impracticable or commercially unprofitable to produce to the maximum amounts.

We are not permitted to stop with this forecast. One of the companies chartered by the legislature of New York and the last so chartered to abstract water from above the Falls, is the Niagara, Lockport & Ontario Power Co. It received in 1894 a franchise without restriction upon the amount of water it might use, but work was to begin in good faith within ten years. It was a modest organization with a slender capital, too slender, as it proved, to begin operations. It did nothing, but in 1904 came to the legislature of New York asking an improved charter enlarging its powers and extending its time. This company proposed to take its water from far above the cataract, as far back as La Salle, and not to return it to the river channel at all, but to carry it off overland by canal to Lock-port, emptying it thence into Lake Ontario. The bill passed the legislature, not without commotion, but encountered trouble in the Executive Chamber. We have referred to the veto of this bill by Governor Odell as a fine act. Perhaps it is not necessary to say more, but the act was done in the face of most turbulent and insistent opposition, and it was clearly actuated by a relentless conviction of the higher rights of the citizens of the state. Ex cathedra statements by special attorneys and the company's engineers that no damage to the scenic features of the Falls could result, were supplemented by an offer of a tremendous sum to the state treasury for the governor's approval. The veto met with almost universal applause throughout the state. This veto was signed May 15, 1904. The company's old charter was signed May 21, 1894. There remained six days in which the company could get to work under its old charter. There is said to be to-day a slender ditch up south of Lockport, the work of a few men and a few carts, which represents the work done in good faith in the six days between May 15 and May 21, 1904. It has become a matter of common knowledge that this company has reorganized since these dates, increasing its capital enormously, and it is also stated that the stock has largely passed from the original organization into the control of one of the great corporations. It now looks as though this company means to do business if the courts have no objection, either under its old charter or with a new one if it can get it. Its intentions and organization are riot a negligible quantity in contemplating what is going to happen to Niagara. Should it succeed in constructing its canal and works it is not likely that with an unrestricted charter the company will consume less than 10,000 cubic feet of water per second, and if we assume this as a fair expression of its mean consumption we must increase the mortgage on the Niagara waters by this amount. It then becomes 58,400 cubic feet per second.

These are then the demands upon the river which are actually in sight.

In the seventh annual report of the Commissioners of the Queen Victoria Niagara Falls Park (1903), Mr. Isham Kandolph, of Chicago, advisory engineer for the commissioners, makes, at the request of the board, a report on the ' Further Development of the Niagara River for Power Purposes,' in which he suggests sites for four additional companies to consume in total 29,996 cubic feet of water per second. We may better construe this proposed abstraction as operations under consideration rather than merely as work suggested. If we add the amount to our last figure the result, 88,396 cubic feet per second, leaves the entire American channel as dry as bone.

Such is the situation. We are out in the open with these figures. They are the figures of the engineers themselves. The counter-argument to these statements has been, so far as the writer's experience goes, either incorrect premises or a rather bored smile. Putting aside entirely the merely proposed developments and considering only those actualy in process we see how closely we are brought to the dead line for the American cataract.

What are we going to do about it? A small, very small proportion of the community in New York and Ontario is content to let the process continue, even to the extinction of Niagara. This element of these communities is largely directly or indirectly concerned with the industrial developments there. Outside the boundaries of these trustee governments this percentage is greatly less. In the country as a whole, speaking for the general intelligent public, the opposition to this procedure seems so overwhelming as to be practically unanimous. New York long ago recognized the necessity of conserving such of these natural beauties as have fallen to her share and the state reservation at Niagara is one of the most beautiful of parks, lamentably small in view of the present encroachment, but upon it she has spent some millions of dollars. The Province of Ontario joined hands in this endeavor and the Queen Victoria Park was once and will be again a beautiful spot, all the more beautiful, the commissioners think, after the installment of the power companies is complete.

The president of the New York Reservation has stated that 800,000 tourists visit the Falls each year. This is a vast number, bringing in an enormous revenue to the place. No other evidence is required to demonstrate how closely the interest of the whole world is focused on Niagara, for these visitors are representatives of every nation. How many hundreds of thousands will seek out Niagara when the world learns that the Delilah of commerce has shorn it of its glory? Will they traverse the seas to behold the wonders of a breakfast-food factory or of any other industrial triumph? These are everywhere; Niagara is unique. To make the problem equable, when will the power developments here put into circulation as many millions of money as do the visitors at the Falls? It is not good business to let the Falls alone?

Commercial Niagara—The Canadian Bank below the Bridge.

There is widespread power throughout the country about Niagara, in central and western New York and in southern Ontario—not in concentrated and overwhelming manifestations, but power is running away now in many a stream which might be developed and stored without offense to the world and with profit to the community. While this power lying at our doors is neglected the apology for the desecration of Niagara lacks the ring of sincerity.

There should be a remedy for every public menace. If there is in the American people, especially in the citizens of New York and Ontario, a sturdy purpose to save Niagara, if it is proposed to meet the problem and solve it, it will be found to possess difficulties enough. The working companies are established in their rights and entirely correct in their demeanor toward the state. The legislature of New York in 1904 memorialized the President upon the subject, urging the initiation of treaty relations with the King of Great Britain having for their purpose the cessation of further abstractions of water. It has been suggested by an influential newspaper that the end may be approached through a presidential commission which shall first determine bow much water may be taken from the river without detracting from the scenic effects. Our figures show plainly and cogently that such procedure is useless because too late. They show that even the existing abstraction of water is qualifying the majesty of the Falls and that the contemplated authorized abstraction will carry the work of destruction well toward its finish. No more franchises are likely to be granted by either of the trustee governments. It may be well if these states or the superior government of each should enter into a treaty agreement to insure this result, but the danger-point being so near, in fact constructively passed, protection for Niagara means control of power production. The hope lies herein, that the companies, either through mechanical limitations, difficulties of cheap production or cheap transportation to a distant market, or through taxation of their product, may not be able to reach the volume of abstraction which is to seriously involve the splendor of the cataract. In this age of marvels, no present mechanical obstacles will long hold sway; the genius of man will overcome them all. In taxation of the power product, not necessarily for revenue but for protection, seems to me to lie the sole means of control of the problem, the only way of saving our national pride before the bar of the world.

## Some Observations on Niagara[3]

It is one of the disadvantages of reading books about natural scenery that they fill the mind with pictures, often exaggerated, often distorted, often blurred, and, even when well drawn, injurious to the freshness of first impressions. Such has been the fate of most of us with regard to the Falls of Niagara. There was little accuracy in the estimates of the first observers of the cataract. Startled by an exhibition of power so novel and so grand, emotion leaped beyond the control of the judgment, and gave currency to notions regarding the water-fall which have often led to disappointment.

A record of a voyage in 1535, by a French mariner named Jacques Cartier, contains, it is said, the first printed allusion to Niagara. In 1603 the first map of the district was constructed by a Frenchman named Champlain. In 1648 the Jesuit Rageneau, in a letter to his superior at Paris, mentions Niagara as "a cataract of frightful height." In the winter of 1678 and 1679 the cataract was visited by Father Hennepin, and described in a book dedicated "to the King of Great Britain." He gives a drawing of the water-fall, which shows that serious changes have taken place since his time. He describes it as "a great and prodigious cadence of water, to which the universe does not offer a

---

[3] Pr John Tyndall

parallel." The height of the fall, according to Hennepin, was more than 600 feet. "The waters," he says, "which fall from this great precipice do foam and boil in the most astonishing manner, making. a noise more terrible than that of thunder. When the wind blows to the south, its frightful roaring may be heard for more than fifteen leagues." The Baron la Hontan, who visited Niagara in 1687, makes the height 800 feet. In 1721, Charlevoix, in a letter to Madame de Maintenon, after referring to the exaggerations of his predecessors, thus states the result of his own observations: "For my part, after examining it on all sides, I am inclined to think that we cannot allow it less than 140 or 150 feet"—a remarkably close estimate. At that time, viz., a hundred and fifty years ago, it had the shape of a horseshoe, and reasons will subsequently be given for holding that this has been always the form of the cataract from its origin to its present site.

As regards the noise of the cataract, Charlevoix declares the accounts of his predecessors, which, I may say, are repeated to the present hour, to he altogether extravagant. He is perfectly right. The thunders of Niagara are formidable enough to those who really seek them at the base of the Horseshoe Fall; but on the banks of the river, and particularly above the fall, its silence, rather than its noise, is surprising. This arises, in part, from the lack of resonance, the surrounding country being flat, and therefore furnishing no echoing surfaces to reenforce the shock of the water. The resonance from the surrounding rocks causes the Swiss Rouss at the Devil's Bridge, when full, to thunder more loudly than the Niagara.

On Friday, the 1st of November, 1872, just before reaching the village of Niagara Falls, I caught, from the railway-train, my first glimpse of the smoke of the cataract. Immediately after my arrival, I went with a friend to the northern end of the American Fall. It may be that my mood at the time toned down the impression produced by the first aspect of this grand cascade; but I felt nothing like disappointment, knowing, from old experience, that time and close acquaintanceship, the gradual interweaving of mind and Nature, must powerfully influence my final estimate of the scene. After dinner we crossed to Goat Island, and, turning to the right, reached the southern end of the American Fall. The river is here studded with small islands. Crossing a wooden bridge to Luna Island, and clasping a tree which grows near its edge, I looked long at the cataract, which here shoots down the precipice like an avalanche of foam. It grew in power and beauty as I gazed upon it. The channel, spanned by the wooden bridge, was deep, and the river there doubled over the edge of the precipice like the swell of a muscle, unbroken. The ledge here overhangs, the water being poured out far beyond the base of the precipice. A space, called the Cave of the Winds, is thus enclosed between the wall of rock and the cataract.

Goat Island terminates in a sheer dry precipice, which connects the American and the Horseshoe

Falls. Midway between both is a wooden hut, the residence of the guide to the Cave of the Winds, and from the hut a winding staircase, called Biddle's Stair, descends to the base of the precipice. On the evening of my arrival I went down this stair, and wandered along the bottom of the cliff. One well-known factor in the formation and retreat of the cataract was immediately observed. A thick layer of limestone formed the upper portion of the cliff. This rested upon a bed of soft shale, which extended round the base of the cataract. The violent recoil of the water against this yielding substance crumbles it away, undermining the ledge above, which, unsupported, eventually breaks off, and produces the observed recession.

At the southern extremity of the Horseshoe is a promontory, formed by the doubling back of the gorge, excavated by the cataract, and into which it plunges. On the promontory stands a stone building, called the Terrapin Tower, the door of which had been nailed up because of the decay of the staircase within it. Through the kindness of Mr. Townsend, the superintendent of Goat Island, the door was opened for me. From this tower, at all hours of the day, and at some hours of the night, I watched and listened to the Horseshoe Fall. The river here is evidently much deeper than the American branch; and, instead of bursting into foam where it quits the ledge, it bends solidly over and falls in a continuous layer of the most vivid green. The tint is not uniform, but varied, long stripes of deeper hue alternating with bands of brighter color. Close to the ledge over which the water rolls, foam is generated, the light falling upon which, and flashing back from it, is sifted in its passage to and fro, and changed from white to emerald green. Heaps of superficial foam are also formed at intervals along the ledge, and immediately drawn down in long white striæ. Lower down, the surface, shaken by the reaction from below, incessantly rustles into whiteness. The descent finally resolves itself into a rhythm, the water reaching the bottom of the fall in periodic gushes. Nor is the spray uniformly diffused through the air, but is wafted through it in successive veils of gauze-like texture. From all this it is evident that beauty is not absent from the Horseshoe Fall, but majesty is its chief attribute. The plunge of the water is not wild, but deliberate, vast, and fascinating. From the Terrapin Tower, the adjacent arm of the Horseshoe is seen projected against the opposite one, midway down; to the imagination, therefore, is left the picturing of the gulf into which the cataract plunges.

The delight which natural scenery produces in some minds is difficult to explain, and the conduct which it prompts can hardly be fairly criticised by those who have never experienced it. It seems to me a deduction from the completeness of the celebrated Thomas Young, that he was unable to appreciate natural scenery. "He had really," says Dean Peacock, "no taste for life in the country; he was one of those who thought that no one who was able to live in London would be content to live elsewhere." Well, Dr. Young, like Dr. Johnson, had a right to his delights; but I can understand a hesitation to accept them, high as they were, to the exclusion of

> "That o'erflowing joy which Nature yields
> To her true lovers."

To all who are of this mind, the strengthening of desire on my part to see and know Niagara Falls, as far as it is possible for them to be seen and known, will be intelligible.

On the first evening of my visit, I met, at the head of Biddle's Stair, the guide to the Cave of the Winds. He was in the prime of manhood—large, well built, firm and pleasant in mouth and eye. My interest in the scene stirred up his, and made him communicative. Turning to a photograph, he described, by reference to it, a feat which he had accomplished some time previously, and which had brought him almost under the green water of the Horseshoe Fall. "Can you lead me there to-morrow?" I asked. He eyed me inquiringly, weighing, perhaps, the chances of a man of light build and with gray in his whiskers in such an undertaking. "I wish," I added, "to see as much of the fall as can be seen, and where you lead I will endeavor to follow." His scrutiny relaxed into a smile, and he said, "Very well; I shall be ready for you to-morrow."

On the morrow, accordingly, I came. In the hut at the head of Biddle's Stair I stripped wholly, and redressed according to instructions—drawing on two pairs of woollen pantaloons, three woollen jackets, two pairs of socks, and a pair of felt shoes. Even if wet, my guide urged that the clothes would keep me from being chilled, and he was right. A suit and hood of yellow oil-cloth covered all. Most laudable precautions were taken by the young assistant of the guide to keep the water out, but his devices broke down immediately when severely tested.

We descended the stair; the handle of a pitchfork doing in my case the duty of an alpenstock. At the bottom my guide inquired whether we should go first to the Cave of the Winds, or to the Horseshoe, remarking that the latter would try us most. I decided to get the roughest done first, and he turned to the left over the stones. They were sharp and trying. The base of the first portion of the cataract is covered with huge bowlders, obviously the ruins of the limestone ledge above. The water does not distribute itself uniformly among these, but seeks for itself channels through which it pours torrentially. We passed some of these with wetted feet, but without difficulty. At length we came to the side of a more formidable current. My guide walked along its edge until he reached its least turbulent portion. Halting, he said, "This is our greatest difficulty; if we can cross here, we shall get far toward the Horseshoe."

He waded in. It evidently required all his strength to steady him. The water rose above his loins, and it foamed still higher. He had to search for footing, amid unseen bowlders, against which the torrent rose violently. He struggled and swayed, but he struggled successfully, and finally reached the shallower water at the other side. Stretching out his arm, he said to me, "Now come on." I looked down the torrent as it rushed to the river below, which was seething with the tumult of the cataract. De Saussure recommended the inspection of Alpine dangers with the view of making them familiar to the eye before they are encountered; and it is a wholesome custom, in places of difficulty, to put the possibility of an accident clearly before the mind, and to decide beforehand what ought to be done should the accident occur. Thus wound up in the present instance, I entered the water. Even where it was not more than knee-deep its power was manifest. As it rose around me, I sought to split the torrent by presenting a side to it; but the insecurity of the footing enabled it to grasp the loins, twist me fairly round, and bring its impetus to bear upon the back. Further struggle was impossible; and, feeling my balance hopelessly gone, I turned, flung myself toward the bank I had just quitted, and was instantly swept into shallower water.

The oil-cloth covering was a great incumbrance; it had been made for a much stouter man, and, standing upright after my submersion, my legs occupied the centres of two bags of water. My guide exhorted me to try again. Prudence was at my elbow, whispering dissuasion; but, taking everything into account, it appeared more immoral to retreat than to proceed. Instructed by the first misadventure, I once more entered the stream. Had the alpenstock been of iron it might have helped me; but, as it was, the tendency of the water to sweep it out of my hands rendered it worse than useless. I, however, clung to it by habit. Again the torrent rose, and again I wavered; but, by keeping the left hip well against it, I remained upright, and at length grasped the hand of my leader at the other side. He laughed pleasantly. The first victory was gained, and he enjoyed it. "No traveller," he said, "was ever here before." Soon afterward, by trusting to a piece of drift-wood which seemed firm, I was again taken off my feet, but was immediately caught by a protruding rock.

We clambered over the bowlders toward the thickest spray, which soon became so weighty as to cause us to stagger under its shock. For the most part nothing could be seen; we were in the midst of bewildering tumult, lashed by the water, which sounded at times like the cracking of innumerable whips. Underneath this was the deep, resonant roar of the cataract. I tried to shield my eyes with my hands, and look upward; but the defence was useless. My guide continued to move on, but at a certain place he halted, and desired me to take shelter in his lee and observe the cataract. The spray did not come so much from the upper ledge as from the rebound of the shattered water when it struck the bottom. Hence the eyes could be protected from the blinding shock of the spray, while the line of vision to the upper ledges remained to some extent clear. On looking upward over the guide's shoulder I could see the water bending over the ledge, while the Terrapin Tower loomed fitfully through the intermittent spray-gusts. We were right under the tower. A little farther on, the cataract, after its first plunge, hit a protuberance some way down, and flew from it in a prodigious burst of spray; through this we staggered. We rounded the promontory on which the Terrapin Tower stands, and pushed, amid the wildest commotion, along the arm of the Horseshoe, until the bowlders failed us, and the cataract fell into the profound gorge of the Niagara River.

Here my guide sheltered me again, and desired me to look up; I did so, and could see, as before, the green gleam of the mighty curve sweeping over the upper ledge, and the fitful plunge of the water as the spray between us and it alternately gathered and disappeared. An eminent friend of mine often speaks to me of the mistake of those physicians who regard man's ailments as purely chemical, to be met by chemical remedies only. He contends for the psychological element of cure. By agreeable emotions, he says, nervous currents are liberated which stimulate blood, brain, and viscera. The influence rained from ladies' eyes enables my friend to thrive on dishes which would kill him if eaten alone. A sanative effect of the same order I experienced amid the spray and thunder of Niagara. Quickened by the emotions there aroused, the blood sped exultingly through the arteries, abolishing introspection, clearing the heart of all bitterness, and enabling one to think with tolerance, if not with tenderness, on the most relentless and unreasonable foe. Apart from its scientific value, and purely as a moral agent, the play, I submit, is worth the candle. My companion knew no more of me than that I enjoyed the wildness; but, as I bent in the shelter of his large frame, he said, "I should like to see you attempting to describe all this." He rightly thought it indescribable. The name of this gallant fellow was Thomas Conroy.

We returned, clambering at intervals up and down so as to catch glimpses of the most impressive portions of the cataract. We passed under ledges formed by tabular masses of limestone, and through some curious openings formed by the falling together of the summits of the rocks. At length we found ourselves beside our enemy of the morning. My guide halted for a minute or two, scanning the torrent thoughtfully. I said that, as a guide, he ought to have a rope in such a place; but he retorted that, as no traveller had ever thought of coming there, he did not see the necessity of keeping a rope. He waded in. The struggle to keep himself erect was evident enough; he swayed, but recovered himself again and again. At length he slipped, gave way, did as I had done, threw himself flat in the water toward the bank, and was swept into the shallows. Standing in the stream near its edge, he stretched his arm toward me. I retained the pitchfork handle, for it had been useful among the bowlders. By wading some way in, the staff could be made to reach him, and I proposed his seizing it. "If you are sure," he replied, "that, in case of giving way, you can maintain your grasp, then I will certainly hold you." I waded in, and stretched the staff to my companion. It was firmly grasped by both of us. Thus helped, though its onset was strong, I moved savely across the torrent. All danger ended here. We afterward roamed sociablv among the torrents and bowlders below the Cave of the Winds. The rocks were covered with organic slime which could not have been walked over with hare feet, hut the felt shoes effectually prevented slipping. We reached the cave and entered it, first by a wooden way carried over the bowlders, and then along a narrow ledge to the point eaten deepest into the shale. When the wind is from the south, the falling water, I am told, can be seen tranquilly from this spot; but, when we were there, a blinding hurricane of spray was whirled against us. On the evening of the same day, I went behind the water on the Canada side, which, I confess, struck me, after the experience of the morning, as an imposture.

To complete my knowledge it was necessary to see the fall from the river below it, and long negotiations were necessary to secure the means of doing so. The only boat fit for the undertaking had been laid up for the winter; but this difficulty, through the kind intervention of Mr. Townsend, was overcome. The main one was, to secure oarsmen sufficiently strong and skilful to urge the boat where I wished it to be taken. The son of the owner of the boat, a finely-built young fellow, but only twenty, and therefore not sufficiently hardened, was willing to go; and up the river I was informed there lived another man who could do any thing with the boat which strength and daring could accomplish. He came. His figure and expression of face certainly indicated extraordinary firmness and power. On Tuesday, the 5th of November, we started, each of us being clad in oil-cloth. The elder oarsman at once assumed a tone of authority over his companion, and struck immediately in among the breakers below the American Fall. He hugged the cross freshets instead of striking out into the smoother water. I asked him why he did so, and he replied that they were directed *outward* not *downward*. At times, the struggle to prevent the bow of the boat from being turned by them was very severe.

The spray was in general blinding, but at times it disappeared, and yielded noble views of the fall. The edge of the cataract is crimped by indentations which exalt its beauty. Here and there, a little below the highest ledge, a secondary one jets out; the water strikes it, and bursts from it in huge, protuberant masses of foam and spray. We passed Goat Island, came to the Horseshoe, and worked for a time along the base of it, the bowlders over which Conroy and myself had scrambled a few days previously lying between us and the base. A rock was before us, concealed and revealed at intervals, as the waves passed over it. Our leader tried to get above this rock, first on the outside of it. The water, however, here was in violent motion. The men struggled fiercely, the elder one ringing out an incessant peal of command and exhortation to the younger. As we were just clearing the rock, the bow came obliquely to the surge; the boat was turned suddenly round, and shot with astonishing rapidity down the river. The men returned to the charge, now trying to get up between the half-concealed rock and the bowlders to the left. But the torrent set in strongly through this channel. The tugging was quick and violent, but we made little way. At length seizing a rope, the principal oarsman made a desperate attempt to get upon one of the bowlders, hoping to be able to drag the boat through the channel; but it bumped so violently against the rock, that the man flung himself back, and relinquished the attempt.

We returned along the base of the American Fall, running in and out among the currents which rushed from it laterally into the river. Seen from below, the American Fall is certainly exquisitely beautiful, but it is a mere frill of adornment to its nobler neighbor the Horseshoe. At times we took to the river, from the centre of which the Horseshoe Fall appeared especially magnificent. A streak of cloud across the neck of Mont Blanc can double its apparent height, so here, the green summit of the cataract shining above the smoke of the spray appeared lifted to an extraordinary elevation. Had Hennepin and La Hontan seen the fall from this position, their estimates of the height would have been perfectly excusable.

From a point a little way below the American Fall, a ferry crosses the river in summer to the Canadian side. Below the ferry is a suspension bridge for carriages and foot-passengers, and a mile or two lower down is the railway suspension bridge. Between the ferry and the latter the river Niagara flows unruffled; but at the suspension bridge the bed steepens and the river quickens its motion. Lower down the gorge narrows, and the rapidity and turbulence increase. At the place called the "Whirlpool Rapids" I estimated the width of the river at 300 feet, an estimate confirmed by the dwellers on the spot. When it is remembered that the drainage of nearly half a continent is compressed into this space, the impetuosity of the river's escape through this gorge may be imagined. Had it not been for Mr. Bierstädt, the distinguished photographer of Niagara, I should have quitted the place without seeing these rapids; for this, and for his agreeable company to the spot, I have to thank him. From the edge of the cliff above the rapids, we descended, a little I confess to a climber's disgust, in an "elevator," because the effects are best seen from the water-level.

Two kinds of motion are here obviously active, a motion of translation, and a motion of undulation—the race of the river through its gorge, and the great waves generated by its collision with, and rebound from, the obstacles in its way. In the middle of the river the rush and tossing are most violent; at all events, the impetuous force of the individual waves is here most strikingly displayed. Vast pyramidal heaps leap incessantly from the river, some of them with such energy as to jerk their summits into the air, where they hang suspended as bundles of liquid spherules. The sun shone for a few minutes. At times, the wind, coming up the river, searched and sifted the spray, carrying away the lighter drops, and leaving the heavier ones behind. Wafted in the proper direction, rainbows appeared and disappeared fitfully in the lighter mist. In other directions the common gleam of the sunshine from the waves and their shattered crests was exquisitely beautiful. The complexity of the action was still further illustrated by the fact that in some cases, as if by the exercise of a local explosive force, the drops were shot radially from a particular centre, forming around it a kind of halo.

The first impression, and, indeed, the current explanation of these rapids is, that the central bed of the river is cumbered with large bowlders, and that the jostling, tossing, and wild leaping of the water there are due to its impact against these obstacles. This may be true to some extent, but there is another reason to be taken into account. Bowlders derived from the adjacent cliffs visibly cumber the *sides* of the river. Against these the water rises and sinks rhythmically but violently, large waves being thus produced. On the generation of each wave there is an immediate compounding of the wave-motion with the river-motion. The ridges, which in still water would proceed in circular curves round the centre of disturbance, cross the river obliquely, and the result is that, at the centre, waves commingle which have really been generated at the sides. In the first instance we had a composition of wave-motion with river-motion; here we have the coalescence of waves with waves. Where crest and furrow cross each other, the motion is annulled; where furrow and furrow cross, the river is ploughed to a greater depth; and, where crest and crest aid each other, we have that astonishing leap of the water which breaks the cohesion of the crests, and tosses them shattered into the air. From the water-level the cause of the action is not so easily seen; but from the summit of the cliff the lateral generation of the waves and their propagation to the centre are perfectly obvious. If this explanation be correct, the phenomena observed at the Whirlpool Rapids form one of the grandest illustrations of the principle of *interference*. The Nile "cataract," Mr. Huxley informs me, offers examples of the same action.

At some distance below the Whirlpool Rapids we have the celebrated whirlpool itself. Here the river makes a sudden bend to the northeast, forming nearly a right angle with its previous direction. The water strikes the concave bank with great force, and scoops it incessantly away. A vast basin has been thus formed, in which the sweep of the river prolongs itself in gyratory currents. Bodies and trees which have come over the falls are stated to circulate here for days without finding the outlet. From various points of the cliffs above, this is curiously hidden. The rush of the river into the whirlpool is obvious enough; and, though you imagine the outlet must be visible, if one existed, you cannot find it. Turning, however, round the bend of the precipice to the northeast, the outlet comes into view.

The Niagara season had ended; the chatter of sight-seers had ceased, and the scene presented itself as one of holy seclusion and beauty. I went down to the river's edge, where the weird loneliness and loveliness seemed to increase. The basin is enclosed by high and almost precipitous banks—covered, when I was there, with russet woods. A kind of mystery attaches itself to gyrating water, due perhaps to the fact that we are to some extent ignorant of the direction of its force. It is said that at certain points of the whirlpool pine-trees are sucked down, to be ejected mysteriously elsewhere. The water is of the brightest emerald-green. The gorge through which it escapes is narrow, and the motion of the river swift though silent. The surface is steeply inclined, but it is perfectly unbroken. There are no lateral waves, no ripples with their breaking bubbles to raise a murmur; while the depth is here too great to allow the inequality of the bed to ruffle the surface. Nothing can be more beautiful than this sloping, liquid mirror formed by the Niagara in sliding from the whirlpool.

The green color is, I think, correctly accounted for in the "Hours of Exercise in the Alps." In crossing the Atlantic I had frequent opportunities of testing the explanation there given. Looked properly down upon, there are portions of the ocean to which we should hardly ascribe a trace of blue; at the most a hint of indigo reaches the eye. The water, indeed, is practically *black*, and this is an indication both of its depth and its freedom from mechanically-suspended matter. In small thicknesses water is sensibly transparent to all kinds of light; but, as the thickness increases, the rays of low refrangibility are first absorbed, and after them the other rays. Where, therefore, the water is very deep and very pure, *all* the colors are absorbed, and such water ought to appear black, as no light is sent from its interior to the eye. The approximation of the Atlantic Ocean to this condition is an indication of its extreme purity.

Throw a white pebble into such water; as it sinks it becomes greener and greener, and, before it disappears, it reaches a vivid blue-green. Break such a pebble into fragments, each of these will behave like the unbroken mass; grind the pebble to powder, every particle will yield its modicum of green; and, if the particles be so fine as to remain suspended in the water, the scattered light will be a uniform green. Hence the greenness of shoal water. You go to bed with the black Atlantic around you. You rise in the morning and find it a vivid green; and you correctly infer that you are crossing the bank of Newfoundland. Such water is found charged with fine matter in a state of mechanical suspension. The light from the bottom may sometimes come into play, but it is not necessary. A storm can render the water muddy by rendering the particles too numerous and gross. Such a case occurred toward the close of my visit to Niagara. There had been rain and storm in the upper-lake regions, and the quantity of suspended matter brought down quite extinguished the fascinating green of the Horseshoe.

Nothing can be more superb than the green of the Atlantic waves when the circumstances are favorable to the exhibition of the color. As long as a wave remains unbroken, no color appears, but, when the foam just doubles over the crest like an Alpine snow-cornice, under the cornice we often see a display of the most exquisite green. It is metallic in its brilliancy. But the foam is necessary to its production. The foam is first illuminated, and it scatters the light in all directions; the light which passes through the higher portion of the wave alone reaches the eye, and gives to that portion its matchless color. The folding of the wave, producing, as it does, a series of longitudinal protuberances and furrows, which act like cylindrical lenses, introduces variations in the intensity of the light, and materially enhances its beauty.

We have now to consider the genesis and proximate destiny of the Falls of Niagara. We may open our way to this subject by a few preliminary remarks upon erosion. Time and intensity are the main factors of geologic change, and they are in a certain sense convertible. A feeble force, acting through long periods, and an intense force, acting through short ones, may produce, approximately, the same results. Here, for example, are some stones kindly lent to me by Dr. Hooker. The first examples of the kind were picked up by Mr. Hackworth on the shores of Lyell's Bay, near

Wellington, in New Zealand, and described by Mr. Travers in the Transactions of the New Zealand Institute. Unacquainted with their origin, you would certainly ascribe their forms to human workmanship. They resemble flint knives and spear-heads, being apparently chiselled off into facets with as much attention to symmetry as if a tool guided by human intelligence had passed over them. But no human instrument has been brought to bear upon these stones. They have been wrought into their present shape by the wind-blown sand of Lyell's Bay. Two winds are dominant here, and they in succession urged the sand against opposite sides of the stone; every little particle of sand clipped away its infinitesimal bit of stone, and in the end sculptured these singular forms.

You know that the Sphinx of Egypt is nearly covered up by the sand of the desert. The neck of the Sphinx is partly cut across, not, as I am assured by Mr. Huxley, by ordinary weathering, but by the eroding action of the fine sand blown against it. In these cases Nature furnishes us with hints which may be taken advantage of in art; and this action of sand has been recently turned to extraordinary account in the United States. When in Boston, I was taken by Mr. Josiah Quincy to see the action of the *sand-blast*. A kind of hopper containing fine silicious sand was connected with a reservoir of compressed air, the pressure being variable at pleasure. The hopper ended in a long slit, from which the sand was blown. A plate of glass was placed beneath this slit, and caused to pass slowly under it; it came out perfectly depolished, with a bright opalescent glimmer, such as could only be produced by the most careful grinding. Every little particle of sand urged against the glass, having all its energy concentrated on the point of impact, formed there a little pit, the depolished surface consisting of innumerable hollows of this description. But this was not all. By protecting certain portions of the surface, and exposing others, figures and tracery of any required form could be etched upon the glass. The figures of open ironwork could be thus copied, while wire gauze placed over the glass produced a reticulated pattern. But it required no such resisting substance as iron to shelter the glass. The patterns of the finest lace could be thus reproduced, the delicate filaments of the lace itself offering a sufficient protection.

All these effects have been obtained with a simple model of the sand-hlast devised for me by my assistant. A fraction of a minute suffices to etch upon glass a rich and beautiful lace pattern. Any yielding substance may be employed to protect the glass. By immediately diffusing the shock of the particle, such substances practically destroy the local erosive power. The hand can bear without inconvenience a sand-shower which would pulverize glass. Etchings executed on glass, with suitable kinds of ink, are accurately worked out by the sand-blast. In fact, within certain limits, the harder the surface, the greater is the concentration of the shock, and the more effectual is the erosion. It is not necessary that the sand should be the harder substance of the two; corundum, for example, is much harder than quartz; still, quartz-sand can not only depolish, but actually blow a hole through a plate of corundum. Nay, glass may be depolished by the impact of fine shot; the lead in this case bruising the glass before it has time to flatten and turn its energy into heat.

And here, in passing, we may tie together one or two apparently unrelated facts. Supposing you turn on, at the lower part of this house, a cock which is fed by a pipe from a cistern at the top of the house, the column of water, from the cistern downward, is set in motion. By turning off the cock, this motion is stopped; and, when the turning off is very sudden, the pipe, if not strong, may be burst by the internal impact of the water. By distributing the turning of the cock over half a second of time, the shock and danger of rupture may be entirely avoided. We have here an example of the concentration of energy in *time*. The sand-blast illustrates the concentration of energy in *space*. The action of flint and steel is an illustration of the same principle. The heat required to generate the spark is intense, and the mechanical action, being moderate, must, to produce fire, be in the highest degree concentrated. This concentration is secured by the collision of hard substances. Calc-spar will not supply the place of flint, nor lead the place of steel, in the production of fire by collision. With the softer substances, the *total* heat produced may be greater than with the hard ones, but, to produce the spark, the heat must be intensely *localized*.

But we can go far beyond the mere depolishing of glass; indeed, I have already said that quartz-sand can wear a hole through corundum. This leads me to express my acknowledgments to General Tilghman, who is the inventor of the sand-blast. To his spontaneous kindness I am indebted for these beautiful illustrations of his process. In this plate of glass you find a figure worked out to a depth of $\frac{3}{8}$ of an inch. Here is a second plate $\frac{7}{8}$ of an inch thick, entirely perforated. Here, again, is a circular plate of marble, nearly half an inch thick, through which open-work of the most intricate and elaborate description has been executed. It would probably take many days to perform this work by any ordinary process; with the sand-blast it was accomplished in an hour. So much for the strength of the blast; its delicacy is illustrated by this beautiful example of line-engraving, etched on glass by means of the blast.

This power of erosion, so strikingly displayed when sand is urged by air, will render you better able to conceive its action when urged by water. The erosive power of a river is vastly augmented by the solid matter carried along with it. Sand or pebbles caught in a river-vortex can wear away the hardest rock; "pot-holes" and deep cylindrical shafts being thus produced. An extraordinary instance of this kind of erosion is to be seen in the Val Tournanche, above the village of this name. The gorge at Handeck has been thus cat out. Such water-falls were once frequent in the valleys of Switzerland; for hardly any valley is without one or more transverse barriers of resisting material, over which the river flowing through the valley once fell as a cataract. Near Pontresina, in the Engadine, there is such a case, the hard gneiss being now worn away to form a gorge through which the river from the Morteratsch Glacier rushes. The barrier of the Kirchet, above Meyringen, is also a case in point. Behind it was a lake, derived from the glacier of the Aar, and over the barrier the lake poured its excess of water. Here the rock, being limestone, was in great part dissolved, but, added to this, we had the action of the solid particles carried along by the water, each of which, as it struck the rock, chipped it away like the particles of the sand-blast. Thus, by solution and mechanical erosion, the great chasm of the Fensteraarschlucht was formed. It is demonstrable that the water which flows at the bottoms of such deep fissures once flowed at the level of what is now their edges, and tumbled down the lower faces of the barriers. Almost every valley in Switzerland furnishes examples of this kind; the untenable hypothesis of earthquakes, once so readily resorted to in accounting for these gorges, being now, for the most part, abandoned. To produce the canons of Western America, no other cause is needed than the integration of effects individually infinitesimal.

And now we come to Niagara. Soon after Europeans had taken possession of the country, the conviction appears to have arisen that the deep channel of the river Niagara below the Falls had been excavated by the cataract. In Mr. Bakewell's

"*Introduction to Geology*," the prevalence of this belief has been referred to: it is expressed thus by Prof. Joseph Henry in the Transactions of the Albany Institute: "In viewing the position of the Falls, and the features of the country round, it is impossible not to be impressed with the idea that this great natural race-way has been formed by the continued action of the irresistible Niagara, and that the Falls, beginning at Lewiston, have, in the course of ages, worn back the rocky strata to their present site." The same view is advocated by Mr. Hall, by Sir Charles Lyell, by M. Agassiz, by Prof. Ramsay—indeed, by almost all of those who have inspected the place.

A connected image of the origin and progress of the fall is easily obtained. Walking northward from the village of Niagara Falls by the side of the river, we have, to our left, the deep and comparatively narrow gorge through which the Niagara flows. The bounding cliffs of this gorge are from 300 to 350 feet high. We reach the whirlpool, trend to the northeast, and, after a little time, gradually resume our northward course. Finally, at about seven miles from the present Falls, we come to the edge of a declivity which informs us that we have been hitherto walking on table-land. At some hundreds of feet below us is a comparatively level plain, which stretches to Lake Ontario. The declivity marks the end of the precipitous gorge of the Niagara. Here the river escapes from its steep, mural boundaries, and, in a widened bed, pursues its way to the lake, which finally receives its waters.

The fact that, in historic times, even within the memory of man, the fall has sensibly receded, prompts the question, How far has this recession gone? At what point did the ledge which thus continually creeps backward begin its retrograde course? To minds disciplined in such researches the answer has been, and will be, at the precipitous declivity which crossed the Niagara from Lewiston, on the American, to Queenstown, on the Canadian side. Over this transverse barrier the united affluents of all the upper lakes once poured their waters, and here the work of erosion began. The dam, moreover, was demonstrably of sufficient height to cause the river above it to submerge Goat Island; and this would perfectly account for the finding by Mr. Hall, Sir Charles Lyell, and others, in the sand and gravel of the island, the same fluviatile shells as are now found in the Niagara River higher up. It would also account for those deposits along the sides of the river, the discovery of which enabled Lyell, Hall, and Ramsay, to reduce to demonstration the popular belief that the Niagara once flowed through a shallow valley.

The physics of the problem of excavation, which I made clear to my mind before quitting Niagara, are revealed by a close inspection of the present Horseshoe Fall. Here we see evidently that the greatest weight of water bends over the very apex of the Horseshoe. In a passage in his excellent chapter on Niagara Falls, Mr. Hall alludes to this fact. Here we have the most copious and the most violent whirling of the shattered liquid; here the most powerful eddies recoil against the shale. From this portion of the fall, indeed, the spray sometimes rises, without solution of continuity, to the region of clouds, becoming gradually more attenuated, and passing finally through the condition of true cloud into invisible vapor, which is sometimes reprecipitated higher up. All the phenomena point distinctly to the centre of the river as the place of greatest mechanical energy, and from the centre the vigor of the fall gradually dies away toward the sides. The horseshoe form, with the concavity facing downward, is an obvious and necessary consequence of this action. Right along the middle of the river the apex of the curve pushes its way backward, cutting along the centre a deep and comparatively narrow groove, and draining the sides as it passes them. Hence the remarkable discrepancy between the widths of the Niagara above and below the Horseshoe. All along its course, from Lewiston Heights to its present position, the form of the fall was probably that of a horseshoe; for this is merely the expression of the greater depth, and consequently greater excavating power, of the centre of the river. The gorge, moreover, varies in width as the depth of the centre of the ancient river varied, being narrowest where that depth was greatest.

The vast comparative erosive energy of the Horseshoe Fall comes strikingly into view when it and the American Fall are compared together. The

American branch of the upper river is cut at a right angle by the gorge of the Niagara. Here the Horseshoe Fall was the real excavator. It cut the rock, and formed the precipice over which the American Fall tumbles. But, since its formation, the erosive action of the American Fall has been almost *nil*, while the Horseshoe has cut its way for 500 yards across the end of Goat Island, and is now doubling back to excavate a channel parallel to the length of the island. This point, I have just learned, has not escaped the acute observation of Prof. Ramsay. The river above the fall bends, and the Horseshoe immediately accommodates itself to the bending, following implicitly the direction of the deepest water in the upper stream. The flexibility of the gorge, if I may use the term, is determined by the flexibility of the river-channel above it. Were the Niagara above the fall far more sinuous than it is, the gorge would obediently follow its sinuosities. Once suggested, no doubt geographers will be able to point out many examples of this action. The Zambesi is thought to present a great difficulty to the erosion theory, because of the sinuosity of the chasm below the Victoria Falls. But, had the river been examined before the formation of this sinuous channel, the present zigzag course of the gorge below the fall could, I am persuaded, have been predicted, while the sounding of the present river would enable us to predict the course to be pursued by the erosion in the future.

But, not only has the Niagara River cut the gorge, it has carried away the chips of its own workshop. The shale being probably crumbled, is easily carried away. But at the base of the fall we find the huge bowlders already described, and by some means or other these are removed down the river. The ice which fills the gorge in winter, and which grapples with the bowlders, has been regarded as the transporting agent. Probably it is so to some extent. But erosion acts without ceasing on the abutting points of the bowlders, thus withdrawing their support, and urging them gradually down the river. Solution also does its portion of the work. That solid matter is carried down is proved by the difference of depth between the Niagara River and Lake Ontario, where the river enters it. The depth falls from 12 feet to 20 feet, in consequence of the deposition of solid matter caused by the diminished motion of the river.

In conclusion, we may say a word regarding the proximate future of Niagara. At the date of excavation assigned to it by Sir Charles Lyell, namely, a foot a year, five thousand years will carry the Horseshoe Fall far higher than Goat Island. As the gorge recedes, it will drain, as it has hitherto done, the banks right and left of it, thus leaving a nearly level terrace between Goat Island and the edge of the gorge. Higher up it will totally drain the American branch of the river, the channel of which in due time will become cultivable land. The American Fall will then be transformed into a dry precipice, forming a simple continuation of the cliffy boundary of the Niagara. At the place occupied by the fall at this moment we shall have the gorge enclosing a right angle, a second whirlpool being the consequence of this. To those who visit Niagara five millenniums hence, I leave the verification of this prediction; for my own part, I have a profound persuasion that it will prove literally true.

## The Age of Niagara Falls[4]

Both the interest and the importance of the subject make it worth while to follow out every clew that may lead to the approximate determination of the age of Niagara Falls. During this past season, in connection with some work done for the New York Central Railroad upon their branch line which runs along the eastern face of the gorge from Bloody Run to Lewiston, I fortunately came into possession of data from which an estimate of the age of the falls can be made entirely independent of those which have heretofore been current. The bearing and importance of the new data can best be seen after a brief *résumé* of the efforts heretofore made to solve this important problem.

In 1841 Sir Charles Lyell and the late Prof. James Hall visited the falls together; but, having no means of determining the rate of recession, except from the indefinite reports of residents and guides, they could place no great confidence in the "guess," made by Sir Charles Lyell, that it could not be more than one foot a year. As the length of the gorge from Lewiston up is about seven miles, the time required for its erosion at this rate would be thirty-five thousand years. The great authority and

---
[4] By G. Frederick Wright

popularity of Lyell led the general public to put more confidence in this estimate than the distinguished authors themselves did. Mr. Bakewell, another eminent English geologist, at about the same time estimated the rate of the recession as threefold greater than Lyell and Hall had done, which would reduce the time to about eleven thousand years.

But, to prepare the way for a more definite settlement of the question, the New York Geological Survey, under Professor Hall's direction, had a careful trigonometric survey of the Horseshoe Fall made in 1842, erecting monuments at the points at which their angles were taken, so that, after a sufficient lapse of time, the actual rate of recession could be more accurately determined. In 1886 Mr. Woodward, of the United States Geological Survey, made a new survey, and found that the actual amount of recession in the center of the Horseshoe Fall had proceeded at an average rate of about five feet per annum. The subject was thoroughly discussed by Drs. Pohlman and Gilbert, at the Buffalo meeting of the American Association in 1886, when it was proved, to the satisfaction of every one, that, if the supply of water had been constant throughout its history, the whole work of eroding the gorge from Lewiston to the Falls would have been accomplished, at the present rate of recession, in about seven thousand years.

FIG. 1.—Looking north from below the Whirlpool, showing the electric road at the bottom of the east side of the gorge, and the steam road descending the face about halfway to the top.

But the question was immediately raised, Has the supply of water in Niagara River been constant? It was my privilege, in the autumn of 1892 (see Bulletin of the Geological Society of America, vol. iv, pp. 421-427), to bring forth the first positive evidence that the water pouring over Niagara hail for a time been diverted, having been turned through Lake Nipissing down the valley of the Mattawa into the Ottawa River, following nearly the line of Champlain's old trail and of the present

Canadian Pacific Railroad. The correctness of this inference has been abundantly confirmed by subsequent investigations of Mr. F. B. Taylor and Dr. Robert Bell. The occasion of this diversion of the drainage of the Great Lakes from the Niagara through the Ottawa Valley was the well-known northerly subsidence of the land in Canada at the close of the Glacial period. When the ice melted off from the lower part of the Ottawa Valley the land stood five hundred feet lower than it does now, but the extent of this subsidence diminished both to the south and the west, making it difficult to estimate just how great it was at the Nipissing outlet. A subsidence of one hundred feet at that point, however, would now divert the waters into the Ottawa River. That it actually was so diverted is shown both by converging high-level shore lines at the head of the Mattawa Valley and by the immense delta deposits at its junction with the Ottawa, to which attention was first called in my paper referred to above.

FIG. 2.—View looking east across the gorge near the mouth, showing the railroads and the outcrops of Clinton and Niagara limestones above the steam road.

The indeterminate question which remained was, At what rate did this postglacial elevation of land which has brought it up to its present level proceed? Dr. Gilbert, Professor Spencer, and Mr. Taylor have brought forth a variety of facts which, according to their interpretation, show that this rate of elevation was so slow that from twenty thousand to thirty thousand years was required to restore to the Niagara River its present volume of water. Their arguments are based upon the varying width and depth of the Niagara gorge, proving, as they think, the presence of a smaller amount of water during the erosion of some portions. Dr. Gilbert has also brought forward some facts concerning the extent of supposed erosion produced by the diverted waters of Niagara when passing over an intermediate outlet between Lake Simcoe and Lake Nipissing. But the difficulty of obtaining any safe basis for calculation upon these speculative considerations has increased the desire to find a means of calculation which should be independent of the indeterminate problems involved. That I think I have found, and so have made a beginning in obtaining desired results. *The new evidence lies in the extent of the enlargement of the mouth of the Niagara gorge at Lewiston since the recession of the falls began.*

It is evident that the oldest part of the Niagara gorge is at its mouth, at Lewiston, where the escarpment suddenly breaks down to the level of Lake Ontario. The walls of the gorge rise here to a height of three hundred and forty feet above the level of the river. It is clear that from the moment the recession of the falls began at Lewiston the walls of the gorge on either side have been subject to the action of constant disintegrating agencies, tending to enlarge the mouth and make it V-shaped. What I did last summer was to measure the exact amount of this enlargement, and to obtain an approximate estimate of the rate at which it is going on. As this enlargement proceeds wholly through the action of atmospheric agencies, the conditions are constant, and it is hoped that sufficiently definite results have been obtained to set some limits to the speculations which have been made upon more indefinite grounds.

The face on the east side of the gorge presents a series of alternate layers of hard and soft rocks, of which certain portions are very susceptible to the disintegrating agencies of the atmosphere. The summit consists of from twenty to thirty feet of compact Niagara limestone, which is underlaid by about seventy feet of Niagara shale; which in turn rests upon a compact stratum of Clinton limestone about twenty feet thick, which again is underlaid by a shaly deposit of seventy feet, resting upon a compact stratum of Medina sandstone twenty feet thick, below which a softer sandstone, that crumbles somewhat readily, extends to the level of the river.

The present width of the river at the mouth of the gorge is seven hundred and seventy feet. It is scarcely possible that the original width of the gorge was here any less than this, for in the narrowest places above, even where the Niagara limestone is much thicker than at Lewiston, it is nowhere much less than six hundred feet in width. Nor is it probable that the river has to any considerable extent enlarged its channel at the mouth of the gorge at the water level. On the contrary, it is more probable that the mouth has been somewhat contracted, for the large masses of Niagara and Clinton limestone-and Medina sandstone which have fallen down as the shales were undermined have accumulated at the base as a talus, which the present current of the river is too feeble to remove. This talus of great blocks of hard stone has effectually riprapped the banks, and really encroached to some extent upon the original channel.

FIG. 3.—Looking up the gorge from near Lewiston, showing on the left the exposed situation of the eastern face of the gorge at the extreme angle, where the measurements were made.

We may therefore assume with confidence that the enlargement, under subaerial agencies, of the mouth of the gorge at the top of the escarpment has been no greater than the distance from the present water's edge to the present line of the escarpment at the summit of the Niagara limestone. This we found to be three hundred and eiglity-eight feet—that is, the upper stratum of hard rock on the east side of the gorge had retreated that distance, through the action of atmospheric agencies, since the formation of the gorge first began. The accompanying photogravures and diagram will present the facts at a glance. The total work of enlargement on the east side of the gorge has been the removal of an inverted triangular section of the rock strata three hundred and forty feet high and three hundred and eighty-eight feet base, which would be the same as a rectangular section of one hundred and ninety-four feet base. From this one can readily see that if the average erosion has been at the rate of one quarter of an inch per annum, the whole amount would have fallen down in less than ten thousand years; while if the time is lengthened, as some would have it, to forty thousand years, the rate would be reduced to one sixteenth of an inch per year.

Fortunately, the construction of the railroad along the face of the eastern wall of the gorge affords opportunity to study the rate of erosion during a definite period of time. The accompanying photogravures will illustrate to the eye facts which it is hard to make impressive by words alone. The course of the road is diagonally down the face of the gorge from its summit for a distance of about two miles, descending in that space about two hundred feet to the outcrop of hard quartzose Medina sandstone. The lower mile of this exposure presents the typical situation for making an estimate of the rate at which the face is crumbling away.

Beginning at what used to be known as the "Hermit's Cave," near the Catholic College grounds, where the Niagara shale is well exposed, and extending to the outer limit of the gorge, the height of the face above the railroad averages one hundred and fifty feet. Now, the crumbling away of the superincumbent cliffs gives continual trouble to the road. Three watchmen are constantly employed along this distance to remove the *débris* which falls down, and to give warning if more comes down than they can remove before trains are due. The seventy feet of Niagara shale, and the equal thickness of shaly Medina rock which underlies the Clinton limestone, are constantly falling off, even in fair weather, as anyone can experience by walking along the bank; while after storms, and especially in the spring, when the frost is coming out, the disintegration proceeds at a much more rapid rate. Sometimes two or three days are required by the whole force of section hands to throw over the bank the result of a single fall of material.

At a rate of one quarter of an inch of waste each year the amount of *débris* accumulating for removal on the track along this distance would be only six hundred and ten cubic yards per annum—that is, if six hundred and ten cubic yards of matarial falls down from one mile of the face of the wall where it is a hundred and fifty feet high, the whole amount of enlargement of the mouth of the gorge would be accomplished in less than ten thousand years. Exact accounts have not been kept by the railroad; but even a hasty examination of the face of the wall makes it sure that the actual amount removed has been greatly in excess of six hundred yards annually. This estimate is based partly on the impression of the railroad officials as to the cost of removal, and partly on the impressions of the watchmen who spend their time in keeping guard and in the work of removing it.

FIG. 4.—Nearer view of the upper portion of the face near the mouth, showing the exposure of the situation at that point.

But that is not all. The accompanying photogravures indicate an actual amount of removal over a part of the area enormously in excess of the rate supposed. Fig. 5 shows a portion of the precipice, a hundred feet high, where the road first comes down to the level of the Clinton limestone, and where, consequently, the whole thickness of the Niagara shale is accessible to examination. Fortunately, Patrick MacNamara, the watchman at this station, was a workman on the road at the time of its construction in 1854, and has been connected with the road ever since, having been at his present post for twelve years. We have therefore his distinct remembrance, as well as the appearance of the bank, to inform us where the face of the original excavation then was. In the picture he is standing at the original face, while the other figure is nearly at the back of the space which has been left empty by the crumbling away of the shale. The horizontal distance is fully twenty feet, and the rocks overhang to that amount for the whole distance exposed in the photograph. All this amount of shale has fallen down in forty-four years, making a rate many times larger than the highest we have taken as the basis of our estimate. Of course, tins rate for the crumbling away of the Niagara shale on its fresh exposure is much in excess of the average rate for a long period of time; but it is clear that the rate of erosion at the base of the Niagara limestone at the mouth of the gorge can never have been sufficiently slow to reduce the total average much below the assumed rate of a quarter of an inch a year.

FIG. 5.—Showing extent of erosion at base of the Niagara shale since 1854.
(See description in the text.)

To impress the truth of this statement it is only necessary to follow the progress, in imagination, of the crumbling process which has brought the side of the gorge to its present condition. At first the face of the gorge was perpendicular, the plunging water making the gorge as wide at the bottom as at the top. At successive stages the strata of shale on the side would crumble away, as is shown in our photograph, and undermine the strata of hard rock. The large fragments would fall to the bottom, and, being too large to be carried away by the current, would form the talus to which we have already referred, which would grow in height with every successive century. The actual progress of the enlargement would thus be periodic, and not capable of measurement by decades; but after centuries the progress would be clearly marked, and especially whenever there was a falling away of the lower stratum of compact Medina sandstone, which is about two hundred foot below the top, would a new cycle of rapid disintegrations in the superincumbent strata follow.

An important point to be noticed, and which is evident from two of the reproduced photographs (Figs. 3 and 4), is that the talus has never reached up so high as to check the disintegration at the mouth of the gorge of the Niagara shale and limestone which form the upper one hundred feet of the face, and which exhibit the maximum amount of enlargement which has taken place. The thickness of the Niagara limestone is here so small that it has not been so important an element in forming the talus as it has been farther up the stream, where it is two or three times as thick. Now, while our original supposition was that one quarter of an inch annually was eroded from the upper two hundred feet, this would involve the erosion of a half inch per annum over the top of the gorge to bring the calculation within the limit of ten thousand years. It certainly is difficult for one who examines the facts upon the ground to believe that the crumbling away of this exposed Niagara shale could have been at any less rate than that; so that the estimate of about ten thousand years for the date of that stage of the Glacial period in which Niagara River first began its work of erosion at Lewiston (an estimate which is supported by a great variety of facts independent of those relating to the Niagara gorge) is strongly confirmed by this new line of evidence.

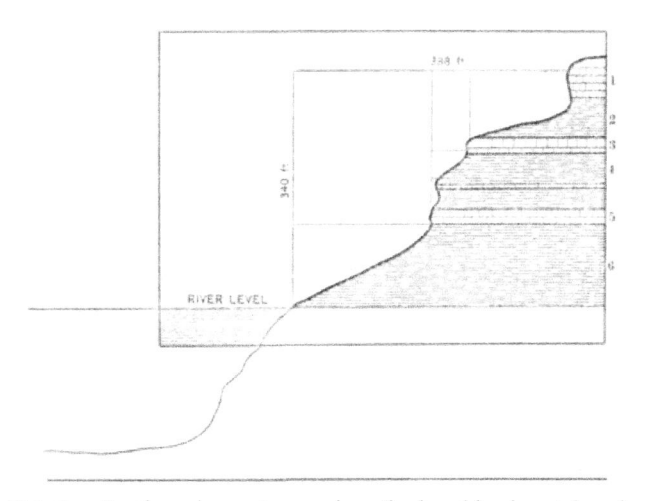

FIG. 6.—Section, drawn to equal vertical and horizontal scale, showing enlargement of Niagara gorge on the east side at its mouth at Lewiston: 1, Niagara limestone, 20 to 30 feet; 2, Niagara shale, 70 feet; 3, Clinton limestone, 20 to 30 feet; 4, Clinton and Medina shale, 70 feet; 5, Quartzose Medina sandstone, 20 to 30 feet; 6, softer Medina sandstone, 120 feet above water level.

So far as I can see, the only question of serious doubt that can be raised respecting this calculation will arise from the possible supposition that, when the eastern drainage over the Niagara channel began, the land stood at such a relatively lower level as would reduce the height of the fall to about half that of the present escarpment at that point; when it might be supposed that a protecting talus had accumulated which would interrupt the lateral erosion for the indefinite period when the drainage was being drawn around by way of the recently opened Lake Nipissing and Mattawa outlet. Then, upon the resumption of the present line of drainage, with the land standing at nearly its present level, the talus may have been undercut, and so fallen down to leave the upper strata exposed as at present. But there does not seem to be sufficient warrant for such a supposition to make it necessary seriously to entertain it, while the objections to it are significant and serious. First, the present narrowness of the river at the water level is such that it does not give much opportunity for enlargement after the first formation of the gorge; secondly, the Niagara limestone at the mouth of the gorge is so thin (stated by Hall to be twenty feet thick) that it would not form a protecting talus, even at half its present height.